SHENANDOAH COLLEGE
LIBRARY
WINCHESTER. VA

DISGUISES

SHENANDOAH COLLEGE
LIBRARY
WINCHESTER. V

DISGUISES

Herbert Scott

University of Pittsburgh Press

Copyright © 1974, Herbert Scott
All rights reserved
Feffer and Simons, Inc., London
Manufactured in the United States of America

Library of Congress Cataloging in Publication Data

Scott, Herbert, birthdate
  Disguises.

  (Pitt poetry series)
  I. Title.
PS3569.C625D5   811'.5'4   73-13316
ISBN 0-8229-5248-3

Some of the poems in this book appeared earlier in the *Beloit Poetry Journal*, *The Blue Guitar*, *Chelsea*, *Epoch*, *Harper's*, *Hearse*, *The Iowa Review*, *Jeopardy*, *Michigan Signatures*, *Perspective*, *Poetry Northwest*, *Poetry Now*, *Poets Kalamazoo*, *SAGE*, and *Westigan Review*. They are reprinted here with the permission of the editors.

"Help Is on the Way" is reprinted from *The Carleton Miscellany*, copyrighted by Carleton College, December 1969.

"Babies" is reprinted from *Just What the Country Needs: Another Poetry Anthology*, by James McMichael and Dennis Saleh. © 1972 by Wadsworth Publishing Company, Inc., Belmont, California 94002.

"For A Woman Whose Fiancé Was Killed at War," "Spring Commences," "The Apprentice Gravedigger," and "You have made fists of your eyes..." are reprinted from *The Massachusetts Review*, © 1967, 1968, 1970 The Massachusetts Review, Inc.

"Passing the Masonic Home for the Aged" and "The Divorcée Looks at Her Son" appeared in the *North American Review* and are copyrighted © 1969 by the University of Northern Iowa.

"Late Fall, Setting Traps" was first published in *Poetry*, December 1969.

"Excavations" first appeared in *The Southern Review*.

PS   Scott, Herbert
3569
.C624   Disguises.
D5
1974
811 Sco84d

*The publication of this book is supported
by a grant from the National Endowment for
the Arts in Washington, D.C., a Federal agency.*

for

Betty and Herbert, my mother and father

Addie Copeland, my grandmother

Contents

I

The Apprentice Gravedigger

The Apprentice Gravedigger

"You'll always have a job."

1

There is a place for every body.
The Rich have frontage on the road;
the Masons sleep together in neat rows;
the Black lean back in weeds,
beyond the grass, where spotted
ground squirrels burrow in their holes.

2

Three feet of dirt,
two of clay,
the last, gray slate
that's hard to chip away.

We dig them clean and straight
as if our lives depended on it.

3

Two buddies
roared their bikes
beneath a cement mixer
and mixed their bodies.

No telling who
was where or what.
They dug out.
I dug them in.

4

The mourners come,
a fluttering of clothes,
in loose formations
through the stones

like birds that search
for scattered seed
on wintered fields.

5

Six months and three hard rains
the boxes go,
the earth caves in.

Wood rots as good
as man, I think.

The ground now knows
its tenant, not by
reputation.

We truck dirt in
and fill the graves again.

6

T.C., Red, and Boomer
pushed me in a grave
and cranked the casket down
till I was flat, laid out,
my hands above my chest.

"White Boy's learning
how to die,"
they laughed and cried,
then pulled me out
and washed my head.

7

We dug one up instead of down.
The widow came to supervise
the moving to a larger plot.

We winched him high. The vault,
expensive moisture-proof cement,
had split. He tipped
and poured himself a drink.

She knew him right enough.
He rained a putrefaction
you could keep.

8

Each time
the same sad words
for stranger bodies,

women cold with fear,
children weeding noses,

husbands wheezing
rumors of death.

9

I killed a king snake sunning
in the branches of a cedar,
cut him with a spade
until he spilled
his breakfast on the grass.

Five sparrow babies,
slick and sweet,
poured out like heavy jam,
the fruit still warm.

I nudged them in the grave.
The snake, the birds, the man,
together in the ground.

10

When it rains
we bury ourselves
in piles of plastic grass,

in the shed,
with straps and shovels,
and visions of the dead.

11

I don't like to dig
the children's graves.
They cramp you in,
not room enough
to swing your axe
or work a sweat.

I'd like to climb in,
brace my back,
and push them longer.
If I was stronger.

12

"What do you do? "
I build holes in the ground.

Winter has come to the old folks' home.
The summer chairs on the porch
are facing the wall, bending
in prayer. Snow hangs

like a shawl across their backs.
On the lawn, weeds grow into drifts,
branches of trees snap
at one another, and do not apologize.

The street has gone away to stay.
Under a roof heavy with clouds, screens creak
like old bones. Inside, the faces
of ten thousand winters press the panes.

Late Fall, Setting Traps

I climb a fever to the forest.
Coyotes creep by my fingers,
possum hang on my breath.

I enter the tongue of a fox,
the oneness of bees,
my mouth puckering
in persimmon whistles.

Beyond the perimeter of motion
ears blame me into silence,
mistletoe gathers the tops of trees.

I set my traps, the creek
freezing at my step.
I won't catch it next spring
when it gallops like deer down its track.

Crow Box

"Come with me," my grandfather said,
"We are going to check the crow box."
Then he took me by the hand and we walked
down to where the lane becomes a ravine.
There on a post was a crude little box
and I had to climb three rungs up the fence
to see the yellow chick enclosed.
"But won't it die? " I asked.
"Bait, my son, one life for ten;
each thing in the proper perspective," he said.

Three mornings I carried oats in my pocket,
water in my hand, to check the crow box,
till the black bird was trapped,
its neck wrung like a chicken's.
An old red hen hatched the next baby chicks
in safety, behind the catalpa tree,
in the high weeds,
and I took four of her brood
in back of the woodshed
and cut off their heads.

Lines on the Ninetieth Birthday of Addie C.

1

The house grows wild
in a density of vegetation,
vines and trees and rain-turned shingles
brown as the earth,
mounted on the hill:
                      Seventy years:
Invisible and not separate from the land,
but letting its roots coil like the vines
where birds are the same birds
infesting like sweet-voiced rats
                      the deadliness of brown
indistinguishable as the house hiding,
the land's keloid;
Rolling before you the fissured fields,
rivulets of years flown down
                      from the high house,
landscapes of trees grown stiff,
the peach and cherry, the elms diseased,
black walnuts webbed with worms which flower
like fruit to take the morning dew;
while high in this festered eye
                      your life wrinkles,
vacant and complete.

2

I picture the young girl.
If beauty is, you were so,
virgin bride in black lace
and formal stance, starched
bones: Handsome girl to bear
the land. You bore children,

raised them to yourself
and watched the land destroy.
And then the husband gone,
the young girl dead of his disease,
You were born and reared
to what your children shaped,
and shared in their growth
as you grew thick and wifely
with no husband but the land.
You gave seed, killed
meat, and bound your hair.

3

I would have known you before,
among the honeysuckle vines,
to touch the bloom, teach and take;
what you were in these young pictures
before you were my blood,
the proud girl in black lace,
a slim life to fashion
in persimmon fields,
      in love-wound rooms.
I would see our daughter grow
to mother me,
image of you when we met
in vague movements against the sky,
the daughter of you
      soon taking your desire.
But you are lost to me,
and so is she.
I cry for my mother born
and my mother bearing me.

4

What is there here to make you stay?
Your pains and fears are what you know.
Pleasures are few, you've outlived growth.
What have you learned?

I never learn, but to adjust.
And now I know you only by your age,
the years you hold to like a walking stick.
The world is older than you ever dreamed:
You've lived to see your sixty-year-old babies die.

Before he died his eyes grew dim
from the old explosion.
But he could still see
to feed himself
and to find the steps before he reached them.
When he would call to us
we would, unmoving, stand upon the lawn
almost laughing through our fingers
as he passed ten feet away.
And one warm Saturday he walked to town
with yellow ribbons in his hair.

The Beekeeper's Wife

She wakes beside his body brown as bees.
Why can't he know? She wonders as she waits
why loneliness must be a private thing.
If she could send the messages she keeps
her hands would tell him of her aching bones,
her mouth would be the only sound he knows.
Outside, the queen is dead, the shifting trees
are warm with bees and ripple with the wind
of wings. Oh she would be the keeper's girl
and run with lifted skirts to gather them,
and hang her heart upon a leaf-blown tree
to house them in, and feed them on her blood.

But could she bear the weight of their blind love?
Some nights she thinks the sound will never stop,
or dreams the bees are netted in her hair.
One day she saw them fill a calf's skull, bring
the bleached bones back to life, become the eyes,
the living tongue that cries. Why can't he see
her body is alive? Why won't he wake
to heal her given wounds? She moves along the bed
and touches him, and waits for him to know
the torture of her fingers, where they go.
There is a fluid movement to his sleep.
She feels his body swarm across the sheet.

For Kyla at One and a Half

"Bless the child."

Your clothes,
unclothed before me,
naked in their emptiness,

are where they fell
when I removed them
half an hour ago.

You left reluctantly,
said NO to sleep,
but slept before

I nestled you in bed.
Our friends have said
you look like me,

have my chin,
my disposition.
I know your *mind's*

your own
as you resist
my mild administration:

You have my stubbornness.
This dress of printed
cotton cloth,

before,
was turning
as you turned,

was learning dizziness,
how to fall
by falling down.

These stockings
poised like doves
about to fly

were white
this afternoon,
in fact were new.

They've learned
the feel of dirt,
the touch of dew.

Lately, we've started
training you,
with no success.

It didn't fit into
your master plan
of what we can

and cannot do.
But you have mastered
how to swing,

the meaning of
a good-night kiss.
You know

the softness of a cat,
the shadow of a leaf,
how silence cannot keep.

Your shoes have found
a silence.
Their mouths are open

shapes you gave to them
and will not speak
until you fill them in.

Tomorrow we will begin
to fill you in.
But I can never teach

what you must learn.
Almost everything I know
I've learned too late.

What can I give you?
These clothes you've shed,
this house,

some words I've found,
my body's warmth,
a way to choose.

The rest
you will discover
as you must,

and you will wear
the shapes your life will spin,
its colors in your hair.

Words for an Older Sister

1

Your face is like I never knew.
Pain runs there
             like messages
We used to send on shingle sailboats
across the pond, or sealed in bottles;
uncorked, we watched them drown.
Or up above the old department store
we watched parades and sent our wishes
down with ticker tape
where heroes rode in black convertibles.
But now the message dies within my head
and no one knows.
                Someone is crying
from dark eyes.

2

The scar is where I cut your leg
on a tin-can lid
strung from a bamboo pole,
whirling, whirling about my head
going fishing for crawdads
your leg was in the way. I cried
and ruined your dress, you know the color,
with blood. I don't,
I don't. How can I tell,
your body turning, turning before my eyes.

3

I see the pulley where you strap your chin.
The weights hang down like heavy hair
        across your back.
You raise them with your neck
to grind the calcium from your spine
and keep your head on straight.

4

They sent you off to Mexico one year.
I almost died. I had to read the Oz books
by myself. Forgot how to play jacks.
Never got past my twos after that.
Pigs in a Basket made me cry. But you came back,
smelling of Spanish leather.

5

The doctor gave you pills to ease the pain.
What numbness you enjoyed
until the pills, the doctor said,
caused erosions other wheres.
And so the pain renews,
a war of pains, uncushioned.
Will this be a thermonuclear engagement?

6

We spent the summer on Grandmother's farm.
You tried to keep me from destroying myself.
Hold on, you said, I'll teach you
how to ride. Instead, I pulled *you* off.
The pony knew I couldn't ride, but you . . .

7

You bled like you would never stop.
The doctor said another child
        would be too much.
I watch you touch my daughter's hair.
Your sons will have no sisters.

8

It was the spring show in the park.
They dressed me in a Philip Morris suit
and put you in the chorus.
I fell asleep and tumbled off the stage.
It stopped the show. But if you laughed
I never knew. I hid my head
against your side the long ride home.

9

I watched your body turn to breasts.
I loved you as a brother
        loves a brother.
Then you became a woman.
        And that is something else.

10

We took our lives to separate places.
I see you now and then,
briefly, not alone, our children
always there. Our words lie clothed and public.
Some things I want to tell you:
I still fall off the horse.
He's bigger now. I'll never learn.

And I still cry for selfish things,
our children, you, myself,
our bodies turning, turning.

Death's Disguises

Excavations

Centuries have passed
since these fires burned in other faces.
Was there dancing then,
lean children in the huts,
deer grazing at the edge of the clearing?
Were antelope hides curing in the wind,
pungent and beautiful?
These drawings on the cliff enlighten us.
We notice here their separation from the tribe,
a cruel winter flight across high mountains.
And here, the murder of a chief,
the sacrificial burning of his wife.

What do we hope to learn?
We spend our summers here, and bring our wives.
There was no great civilization,
no monumental work. They came here, lived,
grew sick, and died. They fed on venison
and squirrel, lay their beds on poplar leaves.
They bound their feet when winter came
and built the snow to keep the wind away.
What decisions did they make?
Where did they miscalculate?
We come with shovels and with sieves
to pan for bones, small hunks of clay, bright beads.

But as we dig we talk of death,
of bodies settling in the ash
of their own fire. And in our tents at night
we gather what we have of what we are,
our bodies, breath, whatever clings,
and learn to wage a kind of love.

The summer wears, the bones collect,
the nights grow cold; we try to resurrect
something from the ashes that we hold.

For a Nun Dead in Africa

It is 87 degrees, humid, the flies
intrude upon her naked body which lies
in the warm dust by the river.
She hears voices like the Mass
and hundreds of bare feet crossing
her life like shadows from the sky.

But first she feels them enter her body.
"It is God's house," she cries.
Her ribs break, releasing
the caught breath, and her breasts are torn.
She doesn't know when they take her arms
and legs and feed them to the river gods.

Sister, I do not know when you will die.
Lumumba lives yet. The ghost of Stanley
walks the jungles. Only last week
Tshombe flew to Paris, Rome, Bonn . . .
but something of you remains, lives here
in the animal night to prove
that we pay in flesh for what we believe.

This morning the widow of a missionary
posed for photographers with her seven
children, smiling. "I know it is part
of God's plan," she said. But there is
no plan. You, innocent exploiter,
have found the living law: the pupil devours
the teacher. This is all we know.

And how can we expect those who are new
beyond hunger and mere survival
to learn what we have never understood?
If it were mine to do, I would forgive.
None of us is exempt from what we are,
for our hate comes before love,
is the birth of love, the incarnation.

                It is not through love
you teach, brave and foolish sister.
It is we who come after,
embittered, sickened in our bones,
who must move into what we have of love.
            There is no time for innocence.

Babies

Our houses are full of babies,
babies under beds, between the pages
of books, in the soup. We open
our mouths and babies march out.
There are babies in our heads
not even born yet. But how we father them!
There are babies in the eyes of lovers
who reach in their thumbs and pull out babies.
And sometimes the world is not ready
and babies pile up, and the streets are full
of babies, and boxes are full of babies,
and sacks and garbage cans,
and broken-down cars are full of babies.
And they are taken home to play with Hunger,
who doesn't play fair and should be sent home
himself, but who wins all the games,
placing himself like a god in the eyes
of those who must worship him.
Or they are taken by the shorter route
and cut off at the pass. And there are babies
for bottles and autopsies, babies for war
and abandonment, and some left over.
There are plenty of babies, no shortages foreseen.
And no peace for the breasts of women.

This piece of sky goes somewhere
above the child's head, the child
with the apple—the sky is blue here,
no clouds in this part of the picture.
But first we must find the child's head.
It is somewhere. We can see the apple,
with the bite missing, in his hand.
But what is this falling like rain?
There are no clouds. Is it tears, or juice
from the apple? We must find the child's head.
He may be hurt. He may need someone
to find his head. And where is the sun?
Let us look for the sun. There are evidences
of it lighting the wings of birds. Somewhere
there must be a sun, and a child's head
with a bite of apple in its mouth.

The Fabulous Frazonis Appear on the Bozo Show

As the curtain parts Pietro is juggling balls,
or heads, or the`embryos of chickens
which disappear into his mouth like shy sparrows.
The young sister, Maria, has circled her body
catching her head between her thighs.
She is hoping someone will find this appealing.
Perhaps she will never marry.

Meanwhile, Rodolpho rides the world's smallest bicycle
which gradually vanishes into his body. He takes
a double take, then rows off the stage
in an imaginary canoe. The audience howls.

Now the Frazonis are climbing to the sky,
a five-headed caterpillar.
The father shoulders his family.
He seems to be saying his back is strong.
His youngest son disappears into the rafters
and is not seen again.

The remaining Frazonis drench their bodies
in gasoline for the finale.
Children all over America ignite their Zippos.
Intricate bone structures are revealed
for an instant, like tableaux on the Fourth of July.

Brilliant teeth promenade in rows,
spastic hands curl into smiles.
Bozo is beside himself. He is too much
for himself, and he splinters
into a thousand vibrations on the laugh-o-meter.

For a Woman Whose Fiancé Was Killed at War

The war has entered you like a lover
Such a flowering there inside you

You are big with war blossoming
You have swallowed the war
The still nights of your body rising in walls.

The war cradled in you cannot get out
It is there and there and there

And your eyes are bees your eyes are watching
The war blooming within you.

I have seen such blossoming:
The oriental games of paper flowers
In the instant of birth becoming bright.

Your eyes are such flowers
The war has reached your eyes your eyes have flowered
And fearful are the flowers of your eyes.

The war has filled you with its dead
You are becoming the war

You are becoming the dead rising within you
And fearful are the colors of the dead.

We will bury you between the pages of a book.
We will bury the image you leave.
We will forget your fragrance.

House Hunting

"He died last week. She's here alone
and wants to sell. You know the way it is."
The realtor pushes in the door, we step inside.

There is a sudden stench that rakes us now,
not death, but death's remains, a smell
that Airwick couldn't hide of stale belongings,

unredeemed beginnings left behind.
The woman sprawls against the couch, her blouse
untucked, an empty glass between her thighs.

We nod and turn away, she doesn't rise.
"Please note the central entry hall."
A gallery of pictures lines the wall.

This one must have been the family long ago,
the man is lean and young, the woman on his arm
must be the woman on the couch,

but smiling then, her children at her skirts.
And here we see him older, striking
a meditative pose. He's looking at some distant place

beyond the scope of what the camera shows.
"There's lots of room. A closet for your coats."
His coats are tightly pressed, like flowers in a book,

unfilled reminders of his form in blacks
and olive tweeds, dark browns. They waft
a rank return of body smells, unbodied ghosts.

He's dead: the closet keeps his clothes alive.
"I'm telling you, I wish I had a house
this nice." The master bedroom, rich brown rug,

an unmade bed, pajamas draped across a chair,
reminds us of a movie set from which
the occupants have left at night, quite suddenly

in great distress, a pipe and tie clasp
on a chest, loose change, a ring, some keys.
"He died last week, was sitting in that chair,

I understand, munching on potato chips."
We look for crumbs beneath our feet.
We note his presence everywhere.

The back porch holds his golf clubs, fishing gear,
a plastic wreath in pliofilm, a case of beer.
We see the dissipation setting in.

"You like this place? There's room to grow."
Some mud-drenched boots. We'd feel too crowded here.
And how can we explain his death

would haunt us here, that in his absence
he would become a member of our family
whose empty place would beckon us

to follow him? Our dreams would fail,
become his dreams gone wrong.
"I'm telling you the truth, this house won't last.

You're close to shopping, schools, and church.
This is an all-white neighborhood."
We live too close to death to move in here.

"Right away, you ought to let me know."
We step outside. The fresh air beats
into our lungs. We nod our heads and go.

We are beginning to discover
the sounds that break our sleep,
which rooms house winds
that blow from nowhere known.
Last night I felt snow
seep into my face,
and listened to the furnace
try to right itself.
By morning, ice glittered
in our eyes,
the children were gone,
perhaps into cupboards
where they hang like mugs,
and birds were napping
in the fireplace,
waiting to be born.
I searched for kindling.
Now we fix our breakfast.
Toast smolders on the grill.
We eat our daily lives.

It is like winter
although the children wade
in mud ponds
and flowers float like birds
across the field.
Winter has been here.
One can see that. Your face
is of winter. I noticed this
before, in that landscape,
after the deep snow,
reflections of coldness,
of clear sky,
before the earth broke through.
The coldness remains
although your hand
turns the fresh soil,
and insects disembark
like explorers from canoes
to search the dark land.

The Drinkers

In this morning light
I think how you seem like my father,
your head skulled on the table
like a bowling ball.
And once in the night
I thought it was a driftwood planter,
pale cactus flowers
blooming from its eyes,
and I thought the movement was an ant.
Old friend, how do you live,
taking no food,
and the wine tasting of salt?
How do you hold on
and every morning bare those wintered gums
to pull another gusher from the jug
and call my name?

Visitation at Borgess Hospital

They are cleaning out the hospital.
402 plays "Exodus" on a ukulele.
Your eyes turn like doorknobs,
opening doors, closing doors.

I can see by your eyes
you won't let him go,
although he has gone already
to the private rooms of death.

In your eyes is a room.
And in that room
an old woman nurses a rat,
a lonely rat nibbling at her breast.
And in its eyes are no rooms.

For Kyla at Three and a Half

1

We planted you in Iowa,
nurtured you in our poor farm
where weeds poisoned animals
and the house shed paint
and washes broke the rubbled road.

We searched the bitter fields
with empty eyes. The drought had come.
And yet you grew.
It was all that we could do
to keep you alive.

And then you came,
like new potatoes from the earth.
I gathered you, and rocked you with the life
you brought. The withered house took root
and bloomed beneath our motion.
Oh lovely food, we fed on you with our rapt hunger.

2

I can almost capture the feel of your body,
the slump of you against my chest.
Yesterday I lifted you to the plane.
Now you sleep in the absence of my arms.

It is dark. Like a vegetable
you grow towards a fresh dawn
and the sun to stretch you awake.

I am awake in your sleep.
Bodies drift across my sight
like abandoned boats
and none of them yours.
Already you have grown beyond my imagining.

3

Of course, you are gone.
The night breeds angels with dark wings.
The hobbled trees latched to the wall
stir and weep.
Your bed flutters like a canceled envelope.

I write you stories, illustrate, and mail them:

Once upon a time, when I was
a boy on Grandmother's farm . . .

And about old Dan, and lots of cats and dogs,
you specify.
Will your mother read them in your eyes?
You spin to sleep.
The night touches me like an omen.

4

Still in the winged sky
when will you come down, my daughter,
step from the plane, child at my feet?

Or will I lie before you
stranger in my death
as you again pass by above me,
wondering at my careful silence,
remembering how childhoods change
with the suddenness of rain?

Centuries pile up between us.
I climb through history,
the wars and celebrations, victories and defeats.
And no hope for peace.

The Friend

When I died my friend came
and railed against the doctors;
and there was much thumbing of eyes,
and ears prancing on my chest.
I remember his tears falling helter-skelter
and his cragged face crumbling like rock.

When I died my friend came
and hid me from undertakers,
a leg behind Milton,
an arm among umbrellas.
And I remember embalmers searching for days,
before it rained and they got me together.

When I died my friend came
and lay in my grave,
cursing the diggers, his words
breaking their backs against the earth.
And I remember his silent weeping,
and darkness dancing on his chest.

I Am a Zoo

Julius Caesar Appears on a Late-Night Talk Show

> *"Are you something of yourself as Julius Caesar?"*
> —a question from the audience

Something, yes. I used to be more
but liked it less. I recall
I was a masochistic fry cook
from Whittier, my arms done
up to the elbows. I love good crisp skin.
I burned like a self-destruct message.

And once I entered from outer space,
the rage that week,
but someone fiddled with my hatch
and I couldn't get back.

You may remember the queer chemist
with a new formula for living.
You begin by shaving your legs.
Or the time I came as a national crisis.
I tightened your belts, didn't I?
You thought I was playing games.
I was dead serious.

But enough of this. I could go on
telling you lies, and you would believe me.
I am something of myself,
but no natural child. I am a zoo.
I am for all the world like you
taking root in the corner of your set.
Listen to me. Quit plotting my suicide.
My people, give me a chance.

The Rapist Speaks to Himself

How difficult to teach these women love.
They claim you force yourself upon them.
Don't they know there is no time
for subtlety? I know the nights
you've cried yourself to sleep.

In the dark you open them like books,
read the braille of their blind lips
and break them into language.
Hear them speak the knowledge of their dying.

Oh no, there is no blame on you.
You are a traveler seeking passage.
You have a message to deliver.
They claim you speak a foreign tongue.
You make them listen.

The Derelict

How fine it is
to wet one's pants,
the sudden warmth
burning like a dream.

How can I explain?

This wine is my family.
I give birth to children
in my bones, their
snug voices singing
to my fingers and my toes.

But one must often let go
of what is best in life.
I grow cold inside.

Good-by, my children.
You die down my legs,
waking me to your going.

My world is a wall of windows.
In the near dark of my mind,
shadows of breasts,
of hands undoing.

I imagine disheveled beds,
a loosening of legs,
that dank, pure spot:
the totems of my faith.

Above me, always,
windows glisten like stars.
I climb the stairs.
A woman, frayed and bare,

comes into the room.
She darkens my sight.
I press too close,
shining in the night.

Across the room
we touch. We feel
our deaths commute
a terrible distance.

The Divorcée Looks at Her Son

In your contrary walk
I hear his footsteps:
he is home from work,
the door closing.
You throw your books on the table.

It is difficult waiting:
what will I see when you enter
this room, your eyes striking my face?
Will it be him, young
as morning, sweet as fresh washed sheets?

You walk into my hands
and in your body I suffer
his desire. But as we touch
you turn within yourself.
You are at odds with me.

I know: he is there,
hiding in your heart.
I put my finger on him.
Where am I? What can I keep?
Why do you look at me like this?

Mozart in Minnesota

Mozart, how you came here
I don't know.

Did you cross on a ship,
in the body of a bird,
as animal, or wheat?

No matter. You made it
to Duluth, where I plow my field,
measure you, and plant your seed.

And now you rise
from your green grave
to take a bow,

surrounded by
an orchestra of sheep,
a worshiping of cows.

Is that your moo, your bleat?
I eat your music with my meat.

The Astronaut

At first I think of my wife,
the way she drank my body in a toast
then said good-by, the letting go;
of that deep pool where I dove for children.
I believed I saw my children
standing in the yard; then countries,
continents, all of Earth.
Now nothing minute is defined.
I am no poet. I have lost Earth.
I think of how it looks like nothing
but a child's painted ball.

Someone imagined me in this universe;
I invent nothing: I open doors, and it is there.
From here I see a spinning disc
that turns my mind,
dark as the soul of matter,
as it plows across fields of space,
and I cannot remember that grave world,
the pull of love, the purge of war.
I could not dream mankind.
In this madhouse womb all is new.
I could not imagine even you.

The Medical Student

Bringing cadavers home from school
can be fun
if you have the right attitude
and a spare bedroom.
Always a good joke on the wife
or the mother-in-law
or that drunk bastard Barney
who felt a strange kinship
to the blonde with the head sawed in half
and invited her home for the weekend.
Barney, I said, stiffs have no feelings.
Barney. Barney?

The Extra

In your background I watch,
sitting on a bench in the park,
my face blossoming in print.
I mix your drinks, my eyes
shining like cubes, and drive
your cab, watching the mirror.
I move the action, sweeping up
after, smoking your cigarettes.
When others cheer, I cheer.
When others starve, I starve.
I am many of a kind. Do not trust me.
I am too much what you have made me.
Watch my eyes. How aware I am
of what is not going on, my voice
ominous and unclear. Sometimes I call
your name, look you in the eye,
and you are surprised at the gun in my hand.

Mother Dear, I am being careful.
My knees chafe as I walk.
I hear them saying: As long
as we are together . . . !
Do not worry. On Sunday
I eat the Lord's body.
Each night I wash my underclothes
and hang them in the dark.
Someone spoke to me in the park
but I did not listen.

You were right to warn me
of those animals. On the street
I feel their eyes follow me
like dogs. I will not feed them.
I have met one nice young man
who reads the Bible, who hopes
to instruct me in passages
I do not understand. He comes
this evening. I hear his knock.
I will finish this letter later.

Help Is on the Way

1 Frankenstein's Wife Writes to Ann Landers

Dear Ann, I think I am losing my husband.
He never straps me to the bed anymore
or fiddles with my parts.
I haven't had a charge in weeks.
Sometimes I think he wants to do me in.
There were intimations of this last week
when I found water in my oil can.
Am I going crazy?
I have faulty wiring and poor compression,
yet he won't fix anything around my body.
Lately, strange arms appeared beneath the couch,
and a leg under the table,
and teeth in my teacup.
I began to put things together.
And finally, last night, he robbed the grave
of that little tramp
who died down the street.
What shall I do?
Should I sever connections?
I would like to make this marriage work.
But where have I failed? I try to keep neat.
Heaven knows it's difficult with no help
in the kitchen, and nothing to wear,
and vapor lock to contend with.
I think I am pregnant, and he won't pay the bills.
What will I do when they turn off the lights?

2 Ann Landers Replies to Frankenstein's Wife

Listen Toots, I've had letters,
but this one takes the cookies.
You are one of a kind.

Did you ever stop to think
the fault may be yours?
You may not have much to work with
but there is no excuse for being run-down.
Shock him with a frilly new nightgown,
set a nice table. It's the little things that count.
Have you checked your breath lately?
Personal hygiene is the ticket, and he'll stop
playing footsie with that leg under the table.
Give the rooster a roost to crow about
and he'll send the other chickens home
is my motto. I don't really think
he is trying to do away with you.
If he does, see a lawyer. If he doesn't,
see a psychiatrist. You may need help.

The Viewer

I watch her perform her consequential acts
for my late-evening pleasure. The scene is Holland,
nineteen forty-one, the message must
go through by hidden radio, tonight,
before the Nazis come. Too late! The bullets
slump into her chest, the earphones stutter
to the floor. I cry, for she is dead again.

No more my wife, if indeed she ever was,
I remember her best in the roles she played:
The young war bride unveils the Sunday door
to innocent disaster. Behold the crumpling face,
the telegram surrendered to the floor.
Or as a paramour, whose sadness tears
my heart, she follows her man from wretched rooms
to dim railway departures, her slim white hands
like tender nurses soothing his tragic face.

I've numbered all her marriages, fifteen.
Does that include my own? I cannot say.
There were five sad love affairs. She died four times,
was ravished twice. The war was cruel: air raids
and concentration camps, one suicide.
Which death was real I never knew,
or if she truly died. It's hard to understand.

At times she makes me laugh, at others, cry.
She's gained a certain versatility
she never had. But the torments are the same.
I watch her making love with subtle grace,
the quickening breath, the ever-loosening face.
Why couldn't she resist? I never learned.
But I no longer think of what we had,
the fragile, failing body of our love.

They taste her mouth. Their fingers on her arm
indent with my desire. I find no substance
in what we were. Nothing but this is real.

The Burial Queen

For Mrs. Emma Smith of Skegness who holds the world's record for being buried alive—100 days, ending September 17, 1968, at Raven's Head, Nottinghamshire, England.

1

Cameras
memorize
my face.

The earth
answers
all questions.

2

It is difficult
to live
with one's self.

Everything
is first
person.

3

My eyes
darken
with time

My ears
silent
as mushrooms

My thoughts
in braille.

4

These hands
comfort my body

feeding
like delicate
deer.

How lonely
I would be
without them!

5

Memory
drowns
in darkness.

I try
to imagine
the sun.

6

Maggots
climb
my face.

Do I carry
their seed
in my flesh?

7

What went wrong?
What am I
doing here?

IV
Moving Out

When I lost my mind
seven health inspectors in silk ties
entered my head.
They liked what they saw and they said:
"This head will do."
But it didn't.

When I lost my mind
seven slum landlords in disguise
entered my head.
They liked what they saw and they said:
"This head will rent."
And it did.

What can I wear?

This typewriter grows heavy
after a long day, and messages
stick to my body, like sweat,
that I must scrub away
before the type sets.
I am bonded, but not erasable.

I do not like the colors of the car this year.
Its two tones clash with my eyes.
It breeds familiarity like flies,
always stopping in the street to shake
someone's body, while I am dreaming
of being alone. I am in the market
for deep maroon or black.

I have tried on every chair in this house.
I wore this bed to work last year.
Someone at the office jumped on me
and didn't bounce. Nothing fits:
the dog, the cat, the radio too loud.
This tailored house: it wears me out.

Churches out of style, last year's marriage,
uniforms of war, and death. It grows late
and I have nothing more to wear.
In these gloves my hands run out.
Children cover me like a shroud.
I hang my mind upon the rack.
I am slipping into something more comfortable.

You have made fists of your eyes.
How they belabor me.
As usual, I mix the drinks.
How many parts?
You play me like a game.

I have lost your openings.
Perhaps they are under the bed.
I don't know. Things are always falling out
of my pockets, friends falling
into strangers, keys losing their locks.

You sip your drink, eyeing your glass
'like a pharmacist measuring drugs.
You used to press a poultice to my lap.

Will you help me look.
I can't find your latch.
We can tell your husband, should he come,
I lost my way in the dark,
saw a light at the door.

But you are in no mood for lies.
You wrote me down. Now scratch me out.
It was not good while it lasted.

When I wake
it is not with myself.
I am an eye opening its head.
I feel behind me a palm
curving like a shell,
a woman's arm, a great stretch of beach,
and mountains I can almost see.
There is a breathing not of me.
I am out in the sea
in the wandering fragments of journeys
lapsing against the sky,
my stomach somewhere in the night
digesting stars.

I walk through your windows.
I know how it is in the bath of your dreams,
soap in your eyes,
visions blurring through bubbles.
I foam at your mouth.

Your body breaks my nose into smell,
your nipples burn in the window like stars.
I know how it is in the wheel of your life.
I will help all I can.

But you don't want out.
You are happy with your lot,
and I am happy for you.

Don't worry about me.
I have squared myself with the sidewalk.
We are on terms. How it mothers me,
keeping my feet dry, helping me home.

Here is my house. It has lost its head.
Rumors are it was suicide.
Don't believe what you read in the papers.

My feet want out. I bend
to deliver them, backward twins.
Hatched from their hard shells
how they wriggle in this new light.

Poor babies. It is not your fault
you have fallen into wrong directions.
They thought they had sized you up,
these shoes pointing like arrows:

    ONE WAY   DO NOT ENTER

How could you obey such rules?
The fools! They kept coming back to that!
They married you to the floor,
waltzed you around the dark,
and stubbed your toes.

Now we have come to this, and you want out.
Stay with me. Keep me company.
They have taken my shoelaces from me.

Snow covers the earth like a uniform,
tracks crossing like berserk buttonholes.
Can I shed these clothes? I walk
in the footsteps of someone coming back.

At the wall I stand like a forked tree,
growing away from myself.
Can I return to the root?
My branches are empty of fruit.

Here, I am the betrayer of flowers. Will I be free
in that woods beyond these fields?
Trees gleam like teeth at its mouth.
Wolves bracket my life with their howls.

This room, I have been here before,
surrounded by the furniture of my mind.
From the ceiling, spiders hang by their tongues.
The pig on the mantel twirls his tail.
I will not oink.

This woman I remember from old movies.
She is the bride of Frankenstein.
I laugh behind these private hands,
surprised that they are mine.

Light creeps round my fingers.
Stay away, I say. Let darkness keep.
Children, indefinite as clay, speak
in omens, their faces bounce like balls.
The doorbell rings. "Friends," the woman says.
I know no friends.
I am a newborn baby left to die.

Why is it always the same,
my soul stretched on the wall
like a skin, the map of my country,
people placed like pins?
Down my streets the invaders come,
the peninsulas of my arms, the heartland gone.
Don't they know that I am a strange country?
They enter me. I am the whore
who eats their seed, my dumb mouth
lost in the realm of language.
How does one speak without interpreters?

How do you tell your body good-by?
If there is much of it, do you miss it more?
Do you say, Look here,
we've had enough of one another.
When I get home tonight
you had best be gone.
Will this work?
Would it be better to leave while sleeping,
a note planted on the pillow like a kiss?
I have known those who favor delusions,
or who forget to bring their bodies home
from work, who reappear in strange cities
                    with new faces.
But it is hard to fool those eyes
opening your mirror each morning.
Can you lose your body in an ocean?
Will it really dissolve in tears?
My grandmother told hers good-by, slowly,
pound by pound, until she had found
a young girl, lost for years in the deepest mountains.
And I have changed my body several times,
that I remember. But each old corpse comes washing back.
And I am running out of trunks, and closets,
and family names, and all my disguises.

PITT POETRY SERIES